Suryia & Roscoe

The True Story of an Unlikely Friendship

Bhagavan "Doc" ANTLE with Thea FELDMAN

Photographs by Barry BLAND

Henry Holt and Company • New York

Henry Holt and Company, LLC
Publishers since 1866
175 Fifth Avenue, New York, New York 10010 [www.HenryHoltKids.com]

Library of Congress Cataloging-in-Publication Data
Antle, Bhagavan.
Suryia and Roscoe : the true story of an unlikely friendship by Bhagavan "Doc" Antle,
with Thea Feldman ; photographs by Barry Bland. — 1st ed.
p.   cm.
Summary: Based on a true story, an orangutan living at a wildlife preserve in South Carolina
forms an unlikely friendship with a lost dog who comes to live there.
ISBN 978-0-8050-9316-2
1. Orangutan—Juvenile fiction. 2. Dogs—Juvenile fiction. [1. Orangutan—Fiction. 2. Dogs—Fiction.
3. Wildlife refuges—Fiction. 4. South Carolina—Fiction.] I. Feldman, Thea. II. Bland, Barry, ill. III. Title.
PZ10.3.A63Su 2011   [E]—dc22   2010025571

First Edition—2011 / Designed by Véronique Lefèvre Sweet
Printed in May 2011 in the United States of America By Worzalla,
Stevens Point, Wisconsin, on acid-free paper. ∞

3 5 7 9 10 8 6 4

To my mother, Merlin,
who inspired my love for all animals
—B. A.

Here is the true story of an amazing friendship between an orangutan named Suryia [SUR-ee-a] and a dog named Roscoe that began at a wildlife preserve in South Carolina.

It was a hot day—a splash-in-the-river day!
Suryia the orangutan and his friend Bubbles the
elephant were on their way to have some fun.

Suryia rode high on Bubbles's back.
Suddenly they heard noises in the woods.
Twigs cracked and leaves crackled.
What was it?

It was a dog! The dog came bursting out of the woods. He was named Roscoe. Suryia and Bubbles had never seen Roscoe before. He was thin and he needed a bath.

Bubbles stopped and stared. But Suryia jumped down and raced toward him.

It isn't often that a dog and an orangutan come face-to-face. They are not usually happy when they do. What happened when Roscoe saw an orange orangutan rushing toward him?

He ran right up to Suryia. And he got a huge, hairy hug!

Suryia hugged Roscoe and smiled.

Roscoe's tail wagged back and forth and back and forth. That was his way of smiling.

Suryia and Roscoe acted just like long-lost friends.

Everyone headed down to the river. *Splash!* Bubbles went in the water. She sprayed them all with her trunk.

Suryia and Roscoe played on the riverbank. They chased each other until Roscoe panted and sat down. Suryia put a long, hairy arm around him. And they rested together.

What happened when Suryia and Bubbles went home?

Roscoe followed them. He sniffed his way up the path and squeezed through the fence.

He saw tigers

and pumas

and lions

and leopards.

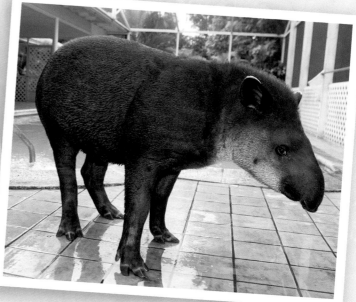

There were gators, turtles,

and tapirs.

And oodles of orangutans!

But where was Suryia?

Sniff, sniff, sniff! Roscoe used his nose to find his friend.

Suryia was having a snack. He offered to share his banana. Did Roscoe like bananas? No! But was Roscoe hungry? Yes!

Suryia offered a bowl of his own food to Roscoe and gave him some water. When Roscoe finished, he wagged his tail.

Roscoe looked like he had been lost for a long time. Everyone tried, but no one could find his owner.

That meant . . .

Roscoe could stay!
He never got lost again.

When Roscoe took a
long walk, Suryia went,
too. Sometimes Bubbles
joined them. Sometimes,
to be silly, Suryia led
Roscoe on a leash.

But in the water, it was Roscoe's turn to lead.
Suryia, like other orangutans, didn't swim, so
he held on to his friend.

When they weren't walking or swimming, they wrestled and rolled. They jumped and tumbled.

They snacked
and snoozed.

And they
smiled a lot.

Even when they were just hanging around, Suryia and Roscoe clearly belonged together!

Author's Note

Suryia and Roscoe live at a wildlife preserve in Myrtle Beach, South Carolina, called T.I.G.E.R.S. (The Institute for Greatly Endangered and Rare Species). The preserve shelters more than a hundred animals and each of them, like Suryia, has a story to tell.

Orangutans such as Suryia once flourished throughout Southeast Asia. Extensive mining and farming—particularly for production of palm oil—have reduced the orangutan's natural habitat to such a tiny area that the orangutan population now numbers only a few thousand. Without intervention, orangutans will go extinct in the wild within the next few years.

Bhagavan "Doc" Antle founded the T.I.G.E.R.S. preserve to provide grassroots support and protection for endangered species. For nearly thirty years, T.I.G.E.R.S. has provided funding, training, and staff to wildlife projects worldwide. The preserve is an initiative of its parent organization, the Rare Species Fund. Visit www.RareSpeciesFund.org for more information about Suryia and Roscoe and the T.I.G.E.R.S. preserve.

In the wild, orangutans are found only in Borneo and Sumatra.

Indonesia

Orangutans' habitat